Appilot/W1

by Bill Martens

Produced by:
Brian Wiser & Bill Martens

 Apple PugetSound Program Library Exchange

Appilot/W1

ISBN: 978-0-359-74408-4

ACKNOWLEDGEMENTS

Appilot/W1 was written entirely by Bill Martens in his mother's home in Roseville Michigan over Christmas break, 1982 and completed on 24 December 1982.

Stephen Gary Wozniak for inventing the Apple II computer. Joff Morgan and Mike Christensen who inspired me to focus and do what it is programmers do. Michael Sly and Jarrod Rominske for the many hours of dedication and fun we had, and of course those with us who labored away on programs in the Brablec computer room in 1982-1983. It was that inspiration which helped me in writing this program. And finally, Samuel Perkins without whose guidance, we would have probably wound up in trouble more than coding.

The cover and book were designed by Brian Wiser.

PRODUCTION

Brian Wiser → Design, Layout, Editing
Bill Martens → Programming, Editing, Documentation

DISCLAIMER

ABOUT BILL MARTENS

Bill Martens is a systems engineer specializing in office infrastructures and has been programming since 1976. The DEC PDP 11/40 with ASR-33 Teletypes and CRT's were his first computing platforms with his first forays in the Apple world coming with the Apple II computer.

Influences in Bill's computing life came from *Byte* magazine, *Creative Computing* magazine, and *Call-A.P.P.L.E.* magazine as well as his mentors Samuel Perkins, Don Williams, Joff Morgan, and Mike Christensen.

Bill is a co-producer of many books including *What's Where in the Apple: Enhanced Edition, The WOZPAK: Special Edition, Nibble Viewpoints: Business Insights From The Computing Revolution,* and co-programmer for the iOS version of the retro game *Structris.* He has written many articles which have appeared in user group newsletters and magazines such as *Call-A.P.P.L.E.*.

Bill worked for Apple Pugetsound Program Library Exchange (A.P.P.L.E.) under Val Golding and Dick Hubert as a data manager and programmer in the 1980s, and is the current president of the A.P.P.L.E. user group established in 1978. He reorganized A.P.P.L.E. and restarted *Call-A.P.P.L.E.* magazine in 2002. He is the production editor for the A.P.P.L.E. website CallApple.org, writes science fiction novels in his spare time, and is a retired semi-pro football player.

ABOUT THE PRODUCERS

Brian Wiser

Brian Wiser is a long-time consultant, enthusiast and historian of Apple, the Apple II and Macintosh. Steve Wozniak and Steve Jobs, as well as *Creative Computing*, *Nibble, InCider*, and *A+* magazines were early influences.

Brian designed, edited, and co-produced many books including: *Nibble Viewpoints: Business Insights From The Computing Revolution*, *Cyber Jack: The Adventures of Robert Clardy and Synergistic Software*, *Synergistic Software: The Early Games*, *The Colossal Computer Cartoon Book: Enhanced Edition*, *What's Where in the Apple: Enhanced Edition*, and *The WOZPAK: Special Edition* – an important Apple II historical book with Steve Wozniak's restored original, technical handwritten notes.

He passionately preserves and archives all facets of Apple's history, and noteworthy related companies such as Beagle Bros and Applied Engineering, featured on AppleArchives.com. His writing, interviews and books are featured on the technology news site CallApple.org and in *Call-A.P.P.L.E.* magazine that he co-produces. Brian also co-produced the retro iOS game *Structris*.

In 2005, Brian was cast as an extra in Joss Whedon's movie *Serenity*, leading him to being a producer and director for the documentary film *Done The Impossible: The Fans' Tale of Firefly & Serenity*. He brought some of the *Firefly* cast aboard his Browncoat Cruise and recruited several of the *Firefly* cast to appear in a film for charity. Brian speaks about his adventures to large audiences at conventions around the country.

TABLE OF CONTENTS

SECTION		PAGE
-----------		-------

CHAPTER 1

Introduction to Appilot/W1

Appilot/W1 is an elementary educational programming language which was written by W. Martens in December of 1982. Pilot was developed by Western Washington University in 1972. Since then there have been many innovations and changes made to Pilot making it more useful for educational purposes.

This version of pilot was written with the teacher and the student in mind. Everything needed to write, edit, and execute Pilot programs are all in one easy to use package. Those users familiar with the Apple II DOS 3.3/Applesoft environment shouldn't have any problems using the Appilot/W1 version 1.0B environment after reading this user's manual. The disk includes the entire Appilot/W1 environment as well as all necessary help files and demo files to get the user started.

Finally, while there are other environments costing outrageous sums of money, our Appilot/W1 system is priced so that everyone can afford it. Should you experience any issues with the floppy disk or the Appilot/ W1 environment, please let us know.

1.1 GETTING STARTED

Getting started with Appilot/W1 is fairly straight forward. To start the Appilot/W1

1

program, place the system diskette into Drive
1 of your Apple II series computer. Then you
can turn on the Apple II or if the computer
is already on and booted, simply type PR#6 to
reboot. After a few seconds, you should see
the following message printed on the display
screen:

LOADING SYSTEM...

This means that the Appilot/W1 system is
being loaded into the computer's memory. The
disk drive will whir for about one minute and
the A.P.P.L.E. logo will appear on the display
screen as shown in the graphic below:

After a few more seconds, the display
screen will clear and the Appilot/W1
programming environment status information will
appear on the display screen:

```
APPILOT / W1 VERSION 1.0B        (C) 24 DEC 1984    BY A.P.P.L.E.
MODE : DOS      SUB-MODE :                 MEMORY : 499    LINES : 0
================================================================
}
```

    At this point, you are ready to begin
using Appilot/W1 and the computer is ready to
accept an Appilot/W1 DOS command (see the help
file for a list of commands). If you type in
a DOS command, it will be executed immediately.
If you type 'HELP' or '?' then you will be
given the appropriate help screen. At the
DOS Prompt, you will be given the DOS Command
Reference for the Appilot/W1 programming
environment.

CHAPTER 2

DOS COMMANDS

Disk Operating System (DOS) commands are commands that tell the computer what to do with the floppy disk. There are a total of 18 commands available in the Appilot/W1 disk operating system (DOS). These commands perform several different tasks. Execute programs, save programs, load programs, edit programs, etc... This documentation will cover all of these commands in depth.

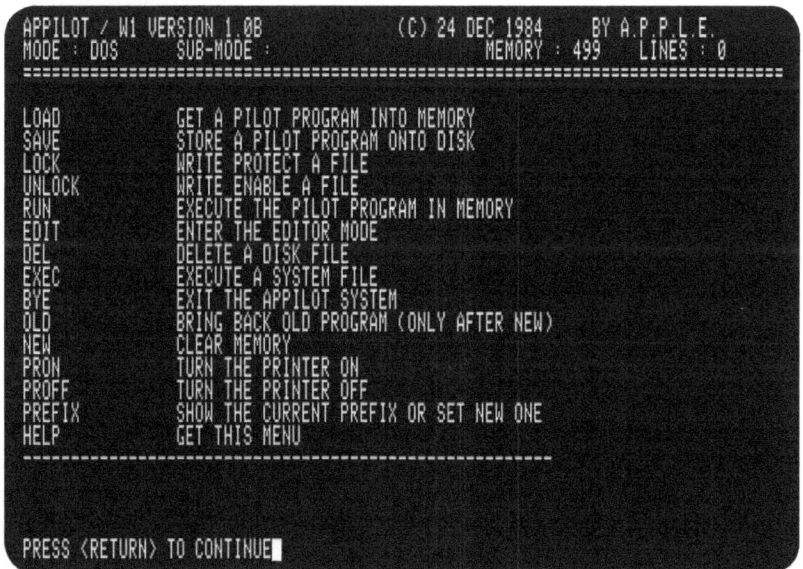

```
APPILOT / W1 VERSION 1.0B        (C) 24 DEC 1984    BY A.P.P.L.E.
MODE : DOS      SUB-MODE :                  MEMORY : 499   LINES : 0
================================================================

LOAD          GET A PILOT PROGRAM INTO MEMORY
SAVE          STORE A PILOT PROGRAM ONTO DISK
LOCK          WRITE PROTECT A FILE
UNLOCK        WRITE ENABLE A FILE
RUN           EXECUTE THE PILOT PROGRAM IN MEMORY
EDIT          ENTER THE EDITOR MODE
DEL           DELETE A DISK FILE
EXEC          EXECUTE A SYSTEM FILE
BYE           EXIT THE APPILOT SYSTEM
OLD           BRING BACK OLD PROGRAM (ONLY AFTER NEW)
NEW           CLEAR MEMORY
PRON          TURN THE PRINTER ON
PROFF         TURN THE PRINTER OFF
PREFIX        SHOW THE CURRENT PREFIX OR SET NEW ONE
HELP          GET THIS MENU
------------------------------------------------------

PRESS <RETURN> TO CONTINUE█
```

2.1 CATALOGING THE DISK

Once you have booted the floppy disk, you will want to see what files are on the disk.

To do this we use the command "CAT", which is short for catalog. You will see a number of files on your new systems disk. A directory listing will be printed out like the following one:

```
APPILOT / W1 VERSION 1.0B        (C) 24 DEC 1984    BY A.P.P.L.E.
MODE : DOS     SUB-MODE :              MEMORY : 499   LINES : 0
================================================================
)CAT


DISK VOLUME 254

 A 003 HELLO
 A 057 APPILOTW1
 T 005 PILOT.HELP.MAIN
 T 003 PILOT.HELP.EDIT
 T 002 DEMO.01.PLT
 A 013 MAKE HELP FILES
 T 005 PILOT.HELP.CMDS

}
```

You now can see what is on the diskette. This can either be mumbo-jumbo to some people or it can be required data for others who understand it.

The PILOT.HELP files are the particular help files for each section of the interpreter and are required to be in the drive whenever the help command is utilized. The interpreter will always revert to the drive that was booted to search for the help files. Thus, if you do not have that disk in the boot drive, the help files will not appear.

The 'PLT' on the end of the file name means that the file is one that was generated and saved by the Pilot interpreter. The numbers beside those codes show how many sectors each file takes up.

6

The word following the number of sectors is the file name. You can't access the system files although you can create them. This is discussed later on in this chapter. To see what is on the diskette in Drive 2, you would type:

CAT2

Conversely, we use 1 with the CAT command to switch the focus back to the first floppy drive on the system.

2.2 SAVING AND LOADING FILES

In order to get access to a Pilot program file which has a prefix of 'PILOT', you must be able to load it. To do this, we use the DOS command 'LOAD' in the following format:

LOAD FILENAME

There must be a space between the command and the filename or there will be an error message printed on the screen. The same applies to all DOS commands that use a filename or a line number with it. The SAVE command is used in the same format as the LOAD command. LOAD will bring a Pilot program file into memory from the disk whereas SAVE takes the present Pilot program file in memory and prints it out to the disk.

There are two DOS commands which go hand in hand with LOAD and SAVE. They are the LOCK and UNLOCK commands.

The LOCK command protects your files
from being accidentally deleted or from being
overwritten. The LOCK command is used in the
following format:

LOCK FILENAME

Where filename is the name of the file
that you wish to protect. To unprotect them
so that you can delete the file or overwrite
the file, use the UNLOCK command. It is used
in the same format as the LOCK command. To
delete the file, use the 'DEL' command. It
is used also in the same format as the LOCK
and UNLOCK command. If you do not include the
file name with each of the commands, an error
message will be displayed on the screen.

2.3 EXECUTING FILES

In order to execute a Pilot program file
you must use the 'RUN' command. This DOS
command tells the computer to execute or run
the Pilot program that is presently in memory.
If there is no program in memory, the computer
will give you an error message. The 'RUN'
command is used in the following format:

RUN

There is no need for a filename. The only
requirement is that you type in a Pilot program
into the computer first or load one in from the
diskette.

8

2.4 EDITING A PROGRAM

The editor of the Appilot/W1 system is
very easy to access and very easy to use. To
enter it, type the following command:

        EDIT

This command will place you at the editor
prompt which looks like this:

        >

From this prompt, you have the following
commands with which to edit your program:

COMMAND   EXPLANATION
---------   -----------------------------------
    D   DELETE LINES
    E   ENTER THE EDITOR INPUT ROUTINE
    I   INSERT LINES
    ?   GET THIS MENU
    Q   QUIT

If you type "E", you are placed at another
prompt that looks like this:

    001_

From here you can begin to type in your
program. To exit, just press the Return key at
the prompt. You can also get the list of Pilot
commands by typing the question mark (?) and
pressing Return.

2.5 EXITING APPILOT/W1

In order to return to BASIC, you would use
the following DOS command:

BYE

This will cause the computer to erase the
memory and reboot the BASIC in the machine.
Caution: be sure you have saved your program
before you exit the system.

CHAPTER 3

PILOT PROGRAMS

This chapter will explain how to type in a Pilot program. It also show how to use some of the DOS commands explained in chapter two with your programs.

3.1 YOUR FIRST PILOT PROGRAM

Here is a small demonstration program for you to type into the Pilot interpreter. It is only a few lines but this is where we start.

```
*:DEMO PROGRAM 1
*:BY W. MARTENS
*:FOR APPLE PILOT/W1
T:THIS IS A TYPE STATEMENT
T:TYPE IN YOUR NAME
A:A$
F:5
T:HELLO THERE ;
T:A$
E:
```

This small program will ask you for your name and then print out a small message with you name at the end of it. The first three lines of the program could be omitted because they have no effect on the interpreter. They are only for documentation purposes.

```
APPILOT / W1 VERSION 1.0B        (C) 24 DEC 1984    BY A.P.P.L.E.
MODE : DOS        SUB-MODE :               MEMORY : 487    LINES : 12
====================================================================

)LIST

001 @ START
002 C:!01=1
003 C:!02=100
004 @ TYPE
005 T:!01;
006 M:!01=!02
007 YJ:END
008 T:' ';
009 C:!01+1
010 J:TYPE
011 @ END
012 E:

}
```

3.2 RUNNING YOUR PROGRAM

After you have typed in the Pilot program,
you want to make sure it is typed exactly like
you want it. To see if it is correct, type the
following command:

    LIST

This DOS command will print your Pilot
program out on the display screen. You can
then compare the program on the screen to the
one in the book. If they are not correct use
the editing commands to correct them. After
you have corrected your program, save it.

You are now ready to execute your program.
To do this we use the following DOS command:

    RUN

```
APPILOT / W1 VERSION 1.0B          (C) 24 DEC 1984    BY A.P.P.L.E.
MODE : DOS      SUB-MODE : RUN               MEMORY : 487   LINES : 12
======================================================================
1,2,3,4,5,6,7,8,9,10,11,12,13,14,15,16,17,18,19,20,21,22,23,24,25,26,27,28,29,30
,31,32,33,34,35,36,37,38,39,40,41,42,43,44,45,46,47,48,49,50,51,52,53,54,55,56,5
7,58,59,60,61,62,63,64,65,66,67,68,69,70,71,72,73,74,75,76,77,78,79,80,81,82,83,
84,85,86,87,88,89,90,91,92,93,94,95,96,97,98,99,100
****DONE****

}
```

Run is also discussed in Chapter 2.   You
program will now begin to execute.

CHAPTER 4

PILOT LANGUAGE COMMANDS

There are many commands in the Pilot
programming language, but we are only going
to discuss the beginning commands in this
Chapter. There are eight commands that are
discussed which will allow you to start writing
your own Pilot programs. Pilot commands are
only one letter long with which two or three
can be combined together to perform complex
operations. All Pilot commands must have
a colon (:) separating the command and the
operators.

4.1 REMARK

The remark statement is used in Pilot
to make your programs readable to anyone who
reads them. This statement is also used for
documentation purposes. It is used in one of
two ways. They are as follows:

    *:COMMENT

Both of these lines perform the same,
but they are both different commands.
Neither command has any effect on the Pilot
interpreter.

4.2 TYPE

The type statement is used to print various things onto the display screen. You can print numbers or text on the screen in the form of variables, strings or even literals. The type statement has several different forms of which only a few are discussed in this section.

The first way the type statement is used is with a literal. It is typed into the interpreter in the following format:

T:THIS IS A LITERAL TYPE

This type statement will type onto the display screen the message that follows the colon(:). The second way to use the type statement is to use a number. You type it like this:

T:569

This will type the number 569 onto the display screen. There are two other very important forms of the type statement that use variables and strings. A variable is a number that represents a number or a computation. A string is a number with a dollar sign($) that represents a literal or several literals depending upon its use. Variables can be from 01 to 99 and strings can be from $01 to $99. The first format is like this:

T:01

This will type whatever the value of variable 01 is on the display screen. The second format is this:

T:$01

This will print whatever literal is represented by $01 onto the display screen. This is just four forms of type discussed in this section. There are several more throughout the rest of the book.

4.3 ACCEPT

The ACCEPT statement in Pilot is used to get input from the keyboard. You can use it to get numeric input or character input or even entire lines of input. You must assign a variable or a string to every accept statement you use. There are only two formats of this statement: one for variables and one for strings. The first format looks like this:

A:01

This will get a numeric input from the user. If a character is input, an error message will appear on the screen. The second format can have any legal type input as long as there are no colons or commas embedded in the input. It looks like this:

A:$01

This will get input and assign it to $01.

4.4A THE LABEL STATEMENT

The LABEL statement is used for creating
a marker within a program for the JUMP command
(4.4b) and the subroutine command (5.1) to
jump to. The LABEL statement makes the
program run at about twice the speed it would
if it referenced line numbers for the JUMP
and SUBROUTINE commands. It is used in the
following format:

@ LABEL NAME

The name of the label can have any
character in it unlike other programming
languages that only allow alphabetic
characters.

4.4B JUMP

The JUMP statement is used to do just
that. Jump around within your Pilot program.
This becomes very useful later on as you
learn more of the advanced Pilot programming
commands. The JUMP statement must have a line
number to jump to. If there is no line number
assigned, an error message will be displayed
on the screen. It is used in the following
format:

J:TYPE ANSWER

This will tell the interpreter to find
label name 'TYPE ANSWER' and continue executing
from that line on, ignoring the previous
line it was on. Be careful not to jump to a

non-existent label, as the computer will give you an error message.

4.5 MATCH

The MATCH statement is used to compare the input from an ACCEPT statement(a) to what should have been input. In this way you can control what is being inputted as your program is executing. The MATCH statement can compare numeric, literal, variable, or string data to what was input. The first format looks like this:

M:56

This will compare the last input to the value 56. The last input does not necessarily have to have been a variable. It could have been a string. The second format looks like this:

M:'MICHIGAN'

This will compare the last string input to the word MICHIGAN. On all compares, a Boolean flag is set. Either the compare will be true if they are the same or false if they are different. The third format is like this:

M:!01 = !02

The number means that it is a variable compare. Without this you will not get the results you want. The fourth and final format of the match statement looks like this:

$$M:\$01 = \$02$$

This will look at $01 and compare it to
$02. After the flags are set, you can use
the yes(y) and no(n) delimiters. They are
discussed in Section 4.8 of this chapter.

4.6 END

The END statement is used to end execution
of your Pilot program. You must always have
an END statement at the end of your program or
you will get an error message. You can have
several within your program but you must have
at least the one at the end of the program.
The END statement is used in the following two
formats:

E:

OR

E:COMMENT

The first format is for those who don't
wish to document their program. The second
format is for those who do wish to make it more
readable.

4.7 COMPUTE

The COMPUTE statement is used to
do mathematical computations or string
manipulation. There are many, many formats of
this statement which number far too many to
cover all of them, but we will give you a basic
outline of the compute statement.

The first part of this is for mathematical computations. If we wanted to figure out what the result of 15*7 was, we would write the compute like this:

```
C:01 = 15
C:02 = 7
C:01 * 02
T:01
```

This would assign variable 01 to equal to 15 and then assign 02 to equal 7. The third line will multiply the two storing the result in 01. It will then print the result on the screen. You can have many computationals within the compute statement. The second format we are going to talk about is string manipulation or concatenating two strings to make one string. To do this we would use the following format:

```
C:$01 = 'HELLO'
C:$02 = ' THERE'
C:$01 + $02
T:$01
E:
```

This program will add the two strings and then print 'HELLO THERE' on the same line.

4.8 YES AND NO DELIMITERS

In the section of this chapter on the match statement, we talked about a Boolean flag. In this chapter we will talk about how to check this flag and put it to use within our Pilot program.

The yes and no delimiters can be used with all of the commands except the delimiter itself. Below is an example of these delimiters in a program:

```
@ START
YT:RIGHT
YJ:RIGHT ANSWER
NT:WRONG
@ RIGHT ANSWER
E:
```

In this program, if the flag is true, it will type the word right and the jump to the end. If the flag is false, then it will print wrong and then end. This can be very useful in educational programs with math especially.

CHAPTER 5

ADVANCED COMMANDS

In this chapter, we will discuss several
commands which will enhance your programs to
make the exciting and easy to use.   There are
many uses for these commands in educational
programs where the student is very young.
It also gives you the power of a high level
language as a programmer.

5.1 SUBROUTINE

The SUBROUTINE command causes the
interpreter to execute an embedded subroutine
within a program.   These subroutines can be
anywhere within the program but be careful not
to mix them up too much or to use too many
subroutines, as the execution of the program
will slow down considerably.

The SUBROUTINE command must always have
line number to jump to. If you forget to
assign the line number, you will get an error
message.   The subroutine command is used in the
following format:

S:SUBROUTINE1
.   .
@ SUBROUTINE1
*:THIS IS THE SUBROUTINE
X:RETURN BACK TO NEXT LINE AFTER SUBROUTINE

The label is a name that you give to that particular line. It is always best to write the program before you actually start typing it into the computer to prevent confusion especially when using the subroutine and jump commands.

5.2 RETURN

The RETURN statement is used to return from the subroutine to the line after the SUBROUTINE command. The RETURN statement is used in the following format:

```
1 S:SUB 1
2 *:THE PROGRAM WILL RETURN HERE
   .
   .
10 @ SUB 1
11 T:IT WORKS!!!!
12 X:
13 E:
```

This is just a sample of how the SUBROUTINE and RETURN commands work within a program.

5.3 INVERSE

The INVERSE command prints out characters on the screen in the opposite background that they are in presently. This command is used to

24

make fancy text display screens. It is used in the following format:

O:

This tells the computer that all text printed hereafter will be in inverse mode.

5.4 NORMAL

The NORMAL command is used to return the printing of text on the screen to the regular text mode. It nullifies both the INVERSE command and the FLASH command. It is used in the following format:

Q:

This tells the interpreter to quit printing in the FLASH mode or the INVERSE mode and to print all following text in the NORMAL mode.

5.5 DELAY

The DELAY command is used to pause execution for a specified period of time. After the specified period of time is done, the program will continue its execution. The DELAY command is used in the following format:

D:5000

The period of time for delay in this command is 5000. The number specified cannot be greater than 32767 and not less than 1. If

the number is out of range, you will get an
error message on the display screen.

5.6 INKEY

     The INKEY command is used to get a single
character of input from the user. After a key
is pressed, the computer will not allow any
more input from the user. The INKEY command is
used with strings. It is used in the following
format:

I:A$

     This will assign A$ to whatever key
is pressed by the user. You can then back
reference A$ and use it later.

APPENDIX A

PILOT COMMAND REFERENCE

COMMAND	EXPLANATION
A:	Get user input from keyboard
C:	Compute
D:	Delay execution for specified amount of time
E:	End execution of pilot program
F:	Flashing text mode
H:	Home cursor
I:	Inkey
J:	Jump to specified line number
M:	Compare user input to the following
O:	Inverse text mode
Q:	Normal text mode
S:	Jump to subroutine at specified line#
T:	Type text to screen
X:	Return from subroutine
Z:	Chain another pilot program
*:	Remarks or comments follow
Y	These two characters are
N	Delimiters for boolean to check flags on input compares

APPENDIX B

DOS COMMAND REFERENCE

COMMAND	EXPLANATION
CAT	Catalog disk directory
LOAD	Get a pilot program into memory
SAVE	Store a pilot program onto disk
LOCK	Write protect a file
UNLOCK	Write enable a file
RUN	Execute the pilot program IN MEMORY
EDIT	Enter the editor mode
DEL	Delete a disk file
EXEC	Execute a system file
BYE	Exit the pilot system
OLD	Bring back old program (only after new)
NEW	Clear memory
PRON	Turn the printer on
PROFF	Turn the printer off
PREFIX	Show the current prefix or set new one
HELP	Get this menu

SOURCE CODE

STARTUP

```
5    REM    ------------------------
10   REM    APPILOT/W1 VER.1.0B
11   REM    STARTUP PROGRAM
12   REM    WRITTEN BY W. MARTENS
13   REM    24 DECEMBER 1982
14   REM    2:34 AM
15   REM    ------------------------
16   REM
20   PRINT   CHR$(4);"RUN APPILOTW1"
```

MAIN SYSTEM

```
1    GOTO 30000
2    PRINT   CHR$ (4)"PR#3"
5    CMD$ = "ACDEHIJMOQSTXZ*YN@"
6    MH$ = "+-*/^="
7    NUM$ = "0123456789"
8    CHK$ = "!$'"
10   D$ =   CHR$(13)+CHR$ (4):DC$= CHR$(4)
11   DX = PEEK(43624)
12   PN = 1: REM  PRINTER SLOT
13   TL = 499: REM   TOTAL MEMORY (LINES)
15   DIM L(99),FL$(99),ER$(20),STCK(20),LBL$(100),
     LBL(100)
20   DIM B$(500),B1$(500),B2$(500),MN$(12)
30   GOSUB 6380
35   GOSUB 9500
40   HOME
130  A = 1
131  MODE$ = "DOS":SB$ = "        ": GOSUB 8000
140  A$ = "": PRINT "}";: GOSUB 7000
```

```
150   IF A$ = "" THEN 140
230   IF A$ = "DATE" THEN 9100
240   IF A$ = "HELP" THEN 6600
241   IF A$ = "?" THEN 6600
250   IF A$ = "PRON" THEN 460
260   IF A$ = "PROFF" THEN 470
270   IF A$ = "PREFIX" THEN 480
280   IF A$ = "CAT" THEN 490
290   IF A$ = "RUN" THEN 1300
300   IF A$ = "LIST" THEN SQ = 1:E9 = A - 1: GOTO 430
310   IF A$ = "NEW" THEN 520
315   IF A$ = "OLD" THEN 5000
320   IF A$ = "BYE" THEN 970
330   IF A$ = "EDIT" THEN 600
338   IF  LEFT$ (A$,3) = "RUN" THEN RF = 1:A$ = ":" +
      A$: GOTO 870
340   IF  LEFT$ (A$,4) = "LOCK" THEN 4570
350   IF  LEFT$ (A$,6) = "UNLOCK" THEN 4620
360   IF  LEFT$ (A$,4) = "SAVE" THEN 770
370   IF  LEFT$ (A$,4) = "LIST" THEN 405
380   IF  LEFT$ (A$,4) = "LOAD" THEN 870
390   IF  LEFT$ (A$,3) = "DEL" THEN 700
395   IF  LEFT$ (A$,3) = "CAT" THEN 502
400   PRINT : PRINT "INVALID COMMAND": PRINT : GOTO 140
405   REM  LIST X    LIST X,    LIST X,Y
410   IF  MID$ (A$,5,1) <  > " " THEN ER = 10: GOTO
      1940
412   A$ =  RIGHT$ (A$, LEN (A$) - 5)
414   IF  RIGHT$ (A$,1) = "," THEN E9 = A - 1:A$ =
      LEFT$ (A$, LEN (A$) - 1): GOSUB 1580:SQ =  VAL
      (A$): GOTO 430
416   FOR X = 1 TO  LEN (A$): IF  MID$ (A$,X,1) = ","
      THEN 420
417   NEXT X: GOSUB 1580:SQ =  VAL (A$):E9 = SQ: GOTO
      430
420   D9$ = A$:TQ = X:A$ =  LEFT$ (D9$,TQ - 1): GOSUB
      1580:SQ =  VAL (A$)
422   A$ =  RIGHT$ (D9$, LEN (D9$) - TQ): GOSUB 1580:E9
      =  VAL (A$)
425   IF SQ < 1 THEN SQ = 1
426   IF E9 > A - 1 THEN E9 = A - 1
```

```
430   REM   *LIST*
431   PRINT
440   IF A = 1 THEN 140
450   FOR X = SQ TO E9:K9$ =  STR$ (X):K9$ = "000" +
      K9$:K9$ =  RIGHT$ (K9$,3): PRINT K9$" "B$(X):
      NEXT X: PRINT : GOTO 140

460   REM   * PRON *
461   MODE$ = "DOS":SB$ = "PRON    ": GOSUB 8000
462   PRINT : PRINT "PRINTER ON": PRINT : PRINT
      D$"PR#"PN: GOTO 140

470   REM   * PROFF *
472   PRINT D$"PR#0": PRINT D$"PR#3":PRINT : PRINT
      "PRINTER OFF": PRINT : GOTO 140

480   REM   * PREFIX *
481   MODE$ = "DOS":SB$ = "PREFIX": GOSUB 8000
482   ONERR  GOTO 6210
483   PRINT D$"PREFIX": INPUT PF$: PRINT "CURRENT
      PREFIX : "PF$: PRINT "NEW PREFIX : ";: GOSUB 7000
484   IF A$ = "" THEN 140
485   PRINT : PRINT D$"PREFIX"A$:PF$ = A$: POKE 216,0:
      GOTO 140
486   PRINT D$"PREFIX"A$: GOTO 140

490   REM   *CAT*
495   ONERR  GOTO 6210
500   CALL 42350: POKE 216,0: PRINT: GOTO 140

502   REM   *CAT PARTICULAR DRIVE *
504   IF LEN (A$)>4 THEN 400
506   DR=VAL(RIGHT$(A$,1))
508   POKE 43624,DR : GOTO 490

520   REM   *NEW*
525   IF A = 1 THEN OL = 0: GOTO 140
530   FOR X = 1 TO A - 1:B1$(X) = B$(X):B$(X) = "":
      NEXT X: B1 = A: OL = 1: HOME : GOTO 130

600   REM   *EDIT*
```

```
602  MODE$ = "EDIT":SB$ = "        ": GOSUB 8000
604  PRINT : PRINT ">";: GOSUB 7000
608  IF A$ = "E" THEN 620
610  IF A$ = "I" THEN 640
612  IF A$ = "D" THEN 660
614  IF A$ = "Q" OR A$ = "" THEN  HOME : GOTO 131
615  IF A$ = "?" THEN 6670
616  PRINT : PRINT "ILLEGAL COMMAND": PRINT : GOTO 604

620  REM  ** EDIT **
622  MODE$ = "EDIT":SB$ = "EDITOR": GOSUB 8000
624  K9$ =  STR$ (A):K9$ = "000" + K9$:K9$ =  RIGHT$
     (K9$,3): PRINT K9$" ";: GOSUB 7000
625  IF A$ = "" THEN 602
626  IF A$ = "HELP" THEN 6650
627  IF A$ = "?" THEN 6650
630  B$(A) = A$:A = A + 1: GOTO 624

640  REM  ** INSERT **
641  MODE$ = "EDIT":SB$ = "INSERT": GOSUB 8000
642  PRINT : PRINT "BEFORE WHICH LINE :";: GOSUB 7000
643  IF A$ = "" THEN  PRINT : GOTO 604
646  A1 =  VAL (A$): IF A1 > A OR A1 < 1 THEN  PRINT :
     PRINT "ILLEGAL LINE NUMBER": PRINT : GOTO 604
647  IF A = A1 THEN 624
648  K9$ =  STR$ (A1):K9$ = "000" + K9$:K9$ =  RIGHT$
     (K9$,3): PRINT K9$" ";: GOSUB 7000
649  IF A$ = "" THEN 604
650  FOR X = A TO A1 + 1 STEP  - 1:B$(X) = B$(X - 1):
     NEXT X
652  B$(A1) = A$:A = A + 1:A1 = A1 + 1: GOTO 648

660  REM  ** DELETE **
661  MODE$ = "EDIT":SB$ = "DELETE": GOSUB 8000
662  PRINT : PRINT "DELETE FROM :";: GOSUB 7000
663  IF A$ = "" THEN 604
664  A2$ = A$: PRINT "        TO :";: GOSUB 7000
665  IF A$ = "" THEN 604
666  A1$ = A$:A$ = A2$:A1 =  VAL (A$): IF A1 < 1
     OR A <  = A1 THEN  PRINT : PRINT "ILLEGAL LINE
     NUMBER": PRINT : GOTO 604
```

```
667   A2 =  VAL (A1$): IF A2 < A1 OR A < = A2 THEN
      PRINT : PRINT "ILLEGAL LINE NUMBER": PRINT : GOTO
      604
668   IF A1 = A2 THEN 680
669   IF A2 = A - 1 THEN A = A - (A2 - A1 + 1): PRINT :
      GOTO 604
670   A3 = A2 - A1 + 1: FOR X = A1 TO A - A3 - 1:B$(X)
      = B$(X + A3): NEXT X:A = A - A3: GOTO 604
680   IF A1 = A - 1 THEN A = A - 1: PRINT : GOTO 604
682   FOR X = A1 TO A - 2:B$(X) = B$(X + 1): NEXT :A =
      A - 1: PRINT : GOTO 604

700   REM  *DEL*
705   ONERR  GOTO 6210
710   IF  MID$ (A$,4,1) < > " " THEN ER = 11: GOTO
      1940
720   PN$ =  RIGHT$ (A$,( LEN (A$) - 4)) + ".PLT"
725   PRINT D$"VERIFY"PN$
730   PRINT D$;"DELETE";PN$
740   PRINT PN$" DELETED": PRINT
750   PRINT
755   POKE 216,0
760   GOTO 140

770   REM  *SAVE*
775   ONERR  GOTO 6230
780   IF  MID$ (A$,5,1) < > " " THEN ER = 11: GOTO
      1940
790   PN$ =  RIGHT$ (A$, LEN (A$) - 5) + ".PLT"
800   PRINT D$;"OPEN";PN$
810   PRINT D$;"WRITE";PN$
820   FOR X = 1 TO (A - 1)
830   FOR Y = 1 TO  LEN (B$(X))
840   PRINT  MID$ (B$(X),Y,1);: NEXT Y: PRINT  CHR$
      (13);: NEXT X
850   IF B$(A - 1) < > "E:" THEN  PRINT "E";".";  CHR$
      (13)
860   PRINT DC$;"CLOSE": POKE 216,0: GOTO 140

870   REM  *LOAD*
875   ONERR  GOTO 6220
```

```
877   IF  LEN (A$) < 5 THEN ER = 11: GOTO 1940
880   IF  MID$ (A$,5,1) <  > " " THEN ER = 11: GOTO
      1940
890   PN$ =  RIGHT$ (A$, LEN (A$) - 5) + ".PLT"
895   PRINT D$;"VERIFY";PN$
900   PRINT D$;"OPEN";PN$: PRINT D$;"READ";PN$
910   A = 1
915   ONERR GOTO 930
917   ZK$ = ""
920   GET A$
922   IF A$ =  CHR$ (13) THEN 930
923   ZK$ = ZK$ + A$:A$ = "": GOTO 920
930   B$(A) = ZK$
935   ONERR GOTO 6220
940   IF LEFT$(ZK$,1) = "E" THEN 960
945   IF LEFT$(ZK$,1) = "E" THEN 960
950   A = A + 1: GOTO 917
960   A = A + 1: PRINT DC$;"CLOSE": POKE 216,0
961   IF RF = 1 THEN RF = 0: A$="":GOTO 1300
965   A$="":GOTO 131

970   REM   *BYE*
980   HOME
990   PRINT "APPLESOFT BASIC"
1000  PRINT "READY"
1010  END
1020  STOP

1280  REM   END OF MONITOR
1290  REM   MONITOR AND INTERPETER BY W. MARTENS (C)
      DEC 1982

1300  REM   RUN
1301  MODE$ = "DOS":SB$ = "RUN    ": GOSUB 8000
1303  GOSUB 9000
1305  POKE  - 16368,0
1310  B = 1
1315  IF A = B THEN 131
1320  F$ = B$(B): POKE 216,0
1325  IF  PEEK ( - 16384) = 155 THEN  POKE  - 16368,0:
      PRINT : GOTO 140
```

```
1330   E$ =  LEFT$ (F$,1)
1350   FOR X = 1 TO 18: IF  MID$ (CMD$,X,1) = E$ THEN
       1370
1360   NEXT X:ER = 4: GOTO 1940
1370   ON X GOTO 1600,5200,4520,2120,3100,3130,3260,33
       30,4270,3810,3860,3900,4220,4290,3830,4240,3700
       ,1710

1400   REM   EXERT BLANK SPACES
1405   ONERR  GOTO 1420
1410   IF  LEFT$ (CK$,1) = " " THEN CK$ =  RIGHT$ (CK$,
       LEN (CK$) - 1): GOTO 1410
1415   RETURN
1420   ER = 11: GOTO 1940

1430   REM   TY$
1435   ONERR  GOTO 1470
1440   TY$ =  LEFT$ (CK$,1)
1450   FOR X = 1 TO 3: IF TY$ =  MID$ (CHK$,X,1) THEN
       1460
1455   NEXT X: IF KK = 1 THEN KL = 1: RETURN
1457   K9 = 10: GOTO 1940
1460   TY = X:K9 = 1: GOSUB 1900: RETURN
1470   ER = 11: GOTO 1940

1480   REM   GET VALUE
1490   ONERR  GOTO 1500
1491   IF  LEN (CK$) = 2 THEN CQ =  VAL (CK$): GOTO
       1498
1492   CQ$ =  LEFT$ (CK$,2):CQ =  VAL (CQ$)
1497   K9 = 2: GOSUB 1900
1498   RETURN
1500   ER = 9: GOTO 1940

1510   REM   GET FUNCTION
1520   MK$ =  LEFT$ (CK$,1)
1530   FOR X = 1 TO 6: IF MK$ =  MID$ (MH$,X,1) THEN
       1550
1540   NEXT X:ER = 6: GOTO 1940
1550   MK = X:K9 = 1: GOSUB 1900: RETURN
1560   REM   GET CK$
```

```
1570   CK$ =  RIGHT$ (F$, LEN (F$) - 2): RETURN

1580   REM   CHECK NUMBER
1590   FOR X = 1 TO  LEN (A$)
1591   FOR Y = 1 TO 10
1592   IF  MID$ (A$,X,1) =  MID$ (NUM$,Y,1) THEN 1597
1593   NEXT Y:ER = 9: GOTO 1940
1597   NEXT X: RETURN

1600   REM   <ACCEPT>
1605   ER = 5: GOSUB 1990:ER = 7
1606   ONERR  GOTO 1960
1608   GOSUB 1560
1610   GOSUB 1400
1620   GOSUB 1430
1625   GOSUB 1400
1630   GOSUB 1480
1640   GOSUB 7000
1645   ER = 7
1646   ONERR  GOTO 1960
1650   ON TY GOTO 1660,1670,1940
1660   GOSUB 1580:FL(CQ) =  VAL (A$): GOTO 1710
1670   FL$(CQ) = A$: GOTO 1710
1710   B = B + 1: GOTO 1320

1900   REM   CK$ EDIT
1910   CK$ =  RIGHT$ (CK$, LEN (CK$) - K9)
1920   IF  LEFT$ (CK$,1) = " " THEN K9 = 1: GOTO 1910
1930   RETURN

1940   REM   ERROR (EXEC)
1950   PRINT : PRINT ER$(ER)" IN LINE "B: PRINT : GOTO
       140
1960   POKE 216,0: GOTO 1940
1990   IF  MID$ (F$,2,1) <  > ":" THEN 1940
2000   RETURN

2120   REM   <END>
2130   PRINT : PRINT "****DONE****": PRINT
2140   GOTO 140
```

```
3100   REM   <HOME>
3110   ER = 5: GOSUB 1990: HOME
3120   GOTO 1710

3130   REM   <INKEY>
3135   ER = 5: GOSUB 1990:ER = 2
3140   GOSUB 1560
3150   IF  LEFT$ (CK$,1) < > "$" THEN  GOTO 1940
3155   ER = 7
3160   GET A$
3170   PRINT A$
3180   K9 = 1: GOSUB 1900
3190   IF  LEN (CK$) < > 2 THEN  GOTO 1940
3200   C9 =  VAL (CK$)
3201   IF C9 < 1 OR C9 > 99 THEN ER = 2: GOTO 1940
3205   GOSUB 1990
3210   FL$(C9) = A$
3220   GOTO 1710

3260   REM   <JUMP>
3270   ER = 5: GOSUB 1990:ER = 8
3275   ONERR  GOTO 1960
3280   GOSUB 1560: GOSUB 1400: IF LL = 0 THEN ER = 12:
       GOTO 1940
3290   FOR X = 1 TO LL: IF CK$ = LBL$(X) THEN B =
       LBL(X): GOTO 1320
3295   NEXT X:ER = 12: GOTO 1940

3330   REM   <MATCH>
3335   ER = 5: GOSUB 1990:ER = 9
3336   ONERR  GOTO 1960
3340   GOSUB 1560
3360   GOSUB 1400: GOSUB 1430
3370   GOSUB 1400: GOSUB 1480
3380   C9 = CQ
3390   GOSUB 1400: GOSUB 1510
3430   ON TY GOTO 3460,3500,1940

3460   REM    VAR.M
3461   ER = 1
3462   IF  LEFT$ (CK$,1) = "!" THEN 3490
```

```
3464 ER = 10: GOTO 1940


3490   REM    VAR.M1
3492   K9 = 1: GOSUB 1900
3494   IF  LEN (CK$) <  > 2 THEN   GOTO 1940
3495   C8 =  VAL (CK$)
3496   IF FL(C9) = FL(C8) THEN FLAG$ = "Y": GOTO 1710
3498   FLAG$ = "N": GOTO 1710


3500   REM   STNG.M
3501   ER = 2
3510   GOSUB 1400: GOSUB 1430
3530   ON TY GOTO 1940,3570,3620


3570   REM    STNG.M1
3580   IF  LEN (CK$) <  > 2 THEN   GOTO 1940
3590   C8 =  VAL (CK$)
3600   IF FL$(C9) = FL$(C8) THEN FLAG$ = "Y": GOTO 1710
3610   FLAG$ = "N": GOTO 1710


3620   REM    LIT.M1
3630   IF  RIGHT$ (CK$,1) <  > "'" THEN   GOTO 1940
3640   CK$ =  LEFT$ (CK$, LEN (CK$) - 1)
3650   IF FL$(C9) = CK$ THEN FLAG$ = "Y": GOTO 1710
3660   FLAG$ = "N": GOTO 1710


3700   REM   <NO>
3710   IF FLAG$ <  > "N" THEN 1710
3720   GOTO 4490


3810   REM   <NORMAL>
3815   ER = 5: GOSUB 1990
3820   NORMAL : GOTO 1710


3830   REM   <REMARK>
3840   ER = 5: GOSUB 1990
3850   GOTO 1710


3860   REM   <SUBROUTINE>
3870   ER = 5: GOSUB 1990:ER = 10
3871   ONERR  GOTO 1960
```

```
3880   GOSUB 1560: GOSUB 1400
3885   ER = 8
3890   IF LL = 0 THEN ER = 12: GOTO 1940
3892   FOR X = 1 TO LL: IF CK$ = LBL$(X) THEN 3897
3895   NEXT X:ER = 12: GOTO 1940
3897   ST = ST + 1: IF ST = 20 THEN  PRINT : PRINT
       "STACK FULL": PRINT : GOTO 140
3898   STCK(ST) = B + 1:B = LBL(X): GOTO 1320

3900   REM  <TYPE>
3905   ER = 5: GOSUB 1990:ER = 10
3907   ONERR  GOTO 1960
3910   GOSUB 1560
3920   GOSUB 1400: GOSUB 1430
3990   IF  RIGHT$ (CK$,1) = ";" THEN HD = 1:CK$ =
       LEFT$ (CK$, LEN (CK$) - 1)
4010   IF TY = 3 THEN  GOTO 4150
4020   IF  LEN (CK$) <  > 2 THEN  GOTO 1940
4030   GOSUB 1400:A$ = CK$: GOSUB 1580:C9 =  VAL (CK$)
4031   IF C9 < 1 OR C9 > 99 THEN 1940
4040   ON TY GOTO 4050,4100

4050   REM   VAR
4051   ER = 1
4060   IF HD = 1 THEN 4080
4070   PRINT FL(C9):HD = 0: GOTO 1710

4080   REM   VARHD
4090   PRINT FL(C9);:HD = 0: GOTO 1710

4100   REM   STNG
4101   ER = 2
4110   IF HD = 1 THEN 4130
4120   PRINT FL$(C9):HD = 0: GOTO 1710

4130   REM    STNG HD
4140   PRINT FL$(C9);:HD = 0: GOTO 1710

4150   REM    LITERAL
4160   IF  RIGHT$ (CK$,1) <  > "'" THEN  GOTO 1940
4170   CK$ =  LEFT$ (CK$, LEN (CK$) - 1)
```

```
4180    IF HD = 1 THEN  GOTO 4200
4190    PRINT CK$:HD = 0: GOTO 1710

4200    REM   LIT HD
4210    PRINT CK$;:HD = 0: GOTO 1710

4220    REM  <RETURN>
4225    IF ST = 0 THEN ER = 13: GOTO 1940
4230    B = STCK(ST):ST = ST - 1: GOTO 1320

4240    REM  <YES>
4250    IF FLAG$ < > "Y" THEN 1710
4260    GOTO 4490
4270    REM  <INVERSE>
4275    ER = 5: GOSUB 1990
4280    INVERSE : GOTO 1710

4290    REM  <CHAIN>
4300    ONERR  GOTO 6230
4302    GOSUB 1990
4305    PN$ =  RIGHT$ (F$,( LEN (F$) - 2)):PN$ = PN$ +
        ".PLT": PRINT D$"VERIFY"PN$
4310    PRINT D$"OPEN"PN$
4320    PRINT D$"READ"PN$
4330    X = 1
4360    ZK$ = ""
4362    GET A$
4364    IF A$ =  CHR$ (13) THEN 4368
4366    ZK$ = ZK$ + A$:A$ = "": GOTO 4360
4368    B$(A) = ZK$
4370    IF ZK$ = "E:" OR ZK$ = "E." THEN 4375
4372    A = A + 1: GOTO 4360
4375    A = A + 1: PRINT DC$;"CLOSE": POKE 216,0: GOTO
        1300

4490    REM   *2ND COMMAND*
4500    F$ =  RIGHT$ (F$, LEN (F$) - 1)
4510    GOTO 1330
4520    REM  <DELAY>
4530    ER = 5: GOSUB 1990
4540    X1 =  VAL ( RIGHT$ (F$, LEN (F$) - 2))
```

```
4550   FOR X = 1 TO X1: NEXT X
4560   GOTO 1710

4570   REM   *LOCK*
4575   ONERR  GOTO 6210
4580   IF  MID$ (A$,5,1) < > " " THEN ER = 11: GOTO
       1940
4590   PN$ =  RIGHT$ (A$, LEN (A$) - 5) + ".PLT"
4595   PRINT D$"VERIFY"PN$
4600   PRINT D$;"LOCK";PN$
4605   POKE 216,0
4610   GOTO 140

4620   REM   *UNLOCK*
4625   ONERR  GOTO 6210
4630   IF  MID$ (A$,7,1) < > " " THEN ER = 11: GOTO
       1940
4635   PRINT D$"VERIFY"PN$
4640   PN$ =  RIGHT$ (A$, LEN (A$) - 7) + ".PLT"
4650   PRINT D$;"UNLOCK";PN$
4655   POKE 216,0
4660   GOTO 140
4670   END

5000   REM   * OLD *
5005   IF OL = 0 THEN  PRINT : PRINT "NO PROGRAM IN
       BUFFER": GOTO 140
5010   FOR X = 1 TO A - 1
5020   B2$(X) = B$(X)
5030   NEXT :B2 = A
5040   FOR X = 1 TO B1 - 1
5050   B$(X) = B1$(X)
5060   NEXT
5070   A = B1
5080   FOR X = 1 TO B2 - 1
5090   B1$(X) = B2$(X):B2$(X) = ""
5100   NEXT
5110   B1 = B2:B2 = 0
5120   PRINT : PRINT "OLD PROGRAM NOW IN MEMORY": PRINT
       : GOTO 131
```

```
5200    REM   <COMPUTE> <C:>
5201    ER = 5: GOSUB 1990:ER = 6
5205    ONERR  GOTO 1960
5210    GOSUB 1560
5220    GOSUB 1400: GOSUB 1430
5270    T9 = TY
5280    GOSUB 1400: GOSUB 1480
5290    C9 = CQ
5291    IF C9 < 1 OR C9 > 99 THEN 1940
5310    GOSUB 1400: GOSUB 1510
5375    KK = 1
5380    GOSUB 1400: GOSUB 1430
5385    KK = 0
5410    IF KL = 0 THEN 5450
5415    KL = 0
5420    FOR X = 1 TO 10
5430    IF TY$ =  MID$ (NUM$,X,1) THEN 5510
5440    NEXT X: GOTO 1940
5450    T7 = TY
5470    IF T7 = 3 THEN  GOTO 5550
5480    IF  LEN (CK$) <  > 2 THEN  GOTO 1940
5490    A$ = CK$: GOSUB 1580:C8 =  VAL (CK$)
5491    IF C8 < 0 OR C8 > 99 THEN 1940
5500    ON T7 GOTO 5700,5840

5510    REM   NUMBER
5511    ER = 9
5520    A$ = CK$: GOSUB 1580:K8 =  VAL (CK$)
5530    IF MK <  > 6 THEN C8 = 0:FL(C8) = K8: GOTO 5700
5540    FL(C9) = K8: GOTO 1710

5550    REM   LITERALS
5560    IF  RIGHT$ (CK$,1) <  > "'" THEN  GOTO 1940
5570    CK$ =  LEFT$ (CK$, LEN (CK$) - 1)
5580    ON MK GOTO 5620,1940,1940,1940,1940,5650

5620    REM   ADD LITERAL
5630    FL$(C9) = FL$(C9) + CK$
5640    GOTO 1710

5650    REM   EQUAL LITERAL
```

```
5660    FL$(C9) = CK$
5670    GOTO 1710


5700    REM    VARIABLE
5701    ER = 3
5710    ON MK GOTO 5720,5740,5760,5780,5800,5820

5720    REM    ADD
5730    FL(C9) = FL(C9) + FL(C8): GOTO 1710

5740    REM    SUBT
5750    FL(C9) = FL(C9) - FL(C8): GOTO 1710

5760    REM    MULT
5770    FL(C9) = FL(C9) * FL(C8): GOTO 1710

5780    REM    DIV
5785    IF FL(C8) = 0 THEN  PRINT : PRINT "DIVISION BY
        ZERO ERROR IN "B: PRINT : GOTO 140
5790    FL(C9) = FL(C9) / FL(C8): GOTO 1710

5800    REM    POWER
5810    FL(C9) = FL(C9) ^ FL(C8): GOTO 1710

5820    REM  EQUAL
5830    FL(C9) = FL(C8): GOTO 1710

5840    REM  STRING
5841    ER = 2
5850    ON MK GOTO 5920,1940,1940,1940,1940,5940
5920    REM    ADD1
5930    FL$(C9) = FL$(C9) + FL$(C8): GOTO 1710

5940    REM    EQL1
5950    FL$(C9) = FL$(C8): GOTO 1710

6200    REM  ERROR (DOS)
6205    PRINT "ERROR AT LINE ";PEEK(218)+256*PEEK(219);"
        IN THE INTERPRETER"
6210    EL = 3: GOTO 6240
6220    EL = 2: GOTO 6240
```

```
6230  EL = 1
6240  ER =  PEEK (222)
6250  IF ER = 4 THEN  PRINT : PRINT  CHR$ (7)"DISK
      WRITE PROTECTED": PRINT : GOTO 6330
6260  IF ER = 5 THEN  PRINT : PRINT  CHR$ (7)"FILE NOT
      FOUND OR EMPTY": PRINT : GOTO 6330
6270  IF ER = 6 THEN  PRINT : PRINT  CHR$ (7)"FILE NOT
      FOUND": PRINT : GOTO 6330
6280  IF ER = 8 THEN  PRINT : PRINT  CHR$ (7)"DISK I/O
      ERROR": PRINT : GOTO 6330
6290  IF ER = 9 THEN  PRINT : PRINT  CHR$ (7)"DISK
      FULL": PRINT : GOTO 6330
6300  IF ER = 10 THEN  PRINT : PRINT  CHR$ (7)"FILE
      LOCKED": PRINT : GOTO 6330
6310  IF ER = 11 THEN  PRINT : PRINT  CHR$ (7)"ILLEGAL
      FILE NAME": PRINT : GOTO 6330
6315  IF ER = 13 THEN  PRINT : PRINT CHRR$(7)"FILE
      TYPE MISMATCH": PRINT : GOTO 6330
6320  PRINT : PRINT  CHR$ (7)"SYSTEM ERROR # "ER"AT
      LOCATION" PEEK (219) * 256 +  PEEK (218)
6330  ON EL GOTO 6340,6350,140
6340  EL$ = "SAVE": GOTO 6360
6350  EL$ = "LOAD"
6360  PRINT DC$"CLOSE": PRINT "UNABLE TO "EL$" "PN$:
      PRINT
6370  POKE 216,0: GOTO 140
6380  FOR X = 1 TO 13: READ ER$(X): NEXT X: RETURN
6390  DATA  "ILLEGAL VARIABLE", "ILLEGAL STRING",
      "ILLEGAL MATHEMATICAL FUNCTION"
6400  DATA  "INVALID COMMAND", "NO COLON (:)
      DELIMETER", "COMPUTATIONAL STATEMENT ERROR"
6410  DATA  "ILLEGAL INPUT STATEMENT","ILLEGAL LINE
      NUMBER", "ILLEGAL VARIABLE OR STRING","SYNTAX
      ERROR"
6420  DATA   "ILLEGAL FILE NAME","LABEL NAME NOT
      FOUND","RETURN WITHOUT A GOSUB"

6500  REM  HELP MODE FOR MAIN MENU
6510  HOME
6515  ONERR  GOTO 6550
6517  PRINT D$;"VERIFY ";F9$;", D";DX
```

```
6520   PRINT D$"OPEN ";F9$
6530   PRINT D$"READ ";F9$
6540   GET A8$: PRINT A8$;
6545   GOTO 6540
6550   PRINT DC$;"CLOSE ";F9$
6560   POKE 216,0
6570   PRINT : PRINT "PRESS <RETURN> TO CONTINUE";: GET
       A$
6575   PRINT : PRINT : ON HL GOTO 140,624,604

6600   F9$ = "PILOT.HELP.CMDS"
6610   HL = 1: GOTO 6500
6650   F9$ = "PILOT.HELP.MAIN"
6660   HL = 2: GOTO 6500
6670   F9$ = "PILOT.HELP.EDIT"
6680   HL = 3: GOTO 6500


7000   REM INPUT ROUTINE
7002   ONERR GOTO 7200
7005   A$ = ""
7010   KEY=PEEK(KB):IF KEY<128 THEN 7010
7015   POKE KS,0:A9$=CHR$(KEY-128)
7020   IF A9$ = "" THEN  RETURN
7040   IF A9$ =  CHR$ (8) THEN 7100
7045   IF A9$ =  CHR$ (13) THEN  PRINT : RETURN
7046   IF A9$ =  CHR$ (21) THEN 7010
7047   IF  LEN (A$) >  = 239 THEN PRINT : RETURN
7048   PRINT A9$;
7050   A$ = A$ + A9$:A9$ = "": GOTO 7010
7100   IF  LEN (A$) < 1 THEN 7010
7105   IF  LEN (A$) = 1 THEN  PRINT A9$;:A$ = "": GOTO
       7010
7110   A$ =  LEFT$ (A$, LEN (A$) - 1): PRINT A9$;: GOTO
       7010

7200   REM ERROR ROUTINE FOR LOAD CRASH
7210   A$=""
7220   GOTO 131 (RETURN??)

8000   REM  TOP OF SCREEN
```

```
8010   TEXT : HOME
8020   VTAB 1: PRINT "APPILOT / W1 VERSION 1.0B
       (C) 24 DEC 1982      BY A.P.P.L.E."
8030   PRINT "MODE : "MODE$,"SUB-MODE : "SB$,"MEMORY :
       "(TL - A) + 1,"LINES : "A - 1
8040   PRINT "========================================
       ===================================="
8050   PRINT
8060   POKE 34,4
8070   RETURN

9000   REM  COMPILE LABEL NAMES
9005   LL = 0: REM   LABEL NAMES RESET
9006   ST = 0: REM    STACK RESET
9010   IF A = 1 THEN   RETURN
9020   FOR X = 1 TO A - 1
9030   IF  LEFT$ (B$(X),1) = "@" THEN 9060
9040   NEXT X
9050   RETURN
9060   IF  MID$ (B$(X),2,1) <  > " " THEN ER = 11: GOTO
       1940
9070   F$ = B$(X): GOSUB 1560:LL = LL + 1
9075   IF LL = 100 THEN   PRINT : PRINT "TOO MANY LABEL
       NAMES": PRINT : GOTO 140
9080   LBL$(LL) = CK$:LBL(LL) = X: GOTO 9040

9100   REM  SET DATE
9102   MODE$ = "DOS":SB$ = "DATE      ": GOSUB 8000
9105   AZ =  PEEK (49040):BZ =  PEEK (49041):CZ =   PEEK
       (49042):DZ =  PEEK (49043)
9110   YR =  INT (BZ / 2)
9120   MN =  INT (AZ / 32) + 8 * (BZ - YR * 2)
9130   DY = AZ -  INT (AZ / 32) * 32
9140   HH = DZ
9150   MM = CZ
9155   IF AZ = 0 OR BZ = 0 THEN  PRINT "<NO DATE>":
       GOTO 9161
9157   IF MM < 10 THEN MM$ = "0" +  STR$ (MM): GOTO
       9160
9158   MM$ =  STR$ (MM)
9160   PRINT "CURRENT DATE & TIME:       "DY"-"MN$(MN)"-
```

```
            "YR"    "HH":"MM$
9161    PRINT
9165    INPUT "CHANGE (Y/N)?";YN$
9167    IF  LEFT$ (YN$,1) <  > "Y" THEN  GOTO 9499
9170    PRINT : PRINT "NEW DATE & TIME:"
9180    INPUT "         YEAR: ";YR
9190    INPUT "        MONTH: ";MN$
9200    INPUT "          DAY: ";DY
9210    INPUT "         HOUR: ";HH
9220    INPUT "       MINUTE: ";MM
9225    IF MM < 10 THEN MM$ = "0" +  STR$ (MM): GOTO
        9230
9227    MM$ =  STR$ (MM)
9230    PRINT : PRINT "NEW DATE & TIME:        "DY"-
        "MN$"-"YR"    "HH":"MM$
9240    PRINT : INPUT "CORRECT (Y/N) ?";YN$
9250    YN$ =  LEFT$ (YN$,1): IF YN$ = "N" THEN  HOME :
        GOTO 9105
9260    FOR X = 1 TO 12: IF MN$ = MN$(X) THEN 9280
9270    NEXT X: PRINT "ILLEGAL MONTH NAME": GET A$: HOME
        : GOTO 9105
9280    IF YR > 99 OR YR < 0 THEN  PRINT "ILLEGAL YEAR
        NAME": GET A$: HOME : GOTO 9105
9290    MN = X
9300    IF HH < 1 OR HH > 12 THEN  PRINT "ILLEGAL HOUR
        #": GET A$: HOME : GOTO 9105
9310    IF MM < 0 OR MM > 59 THEN  PRINT "ILLEGAL MINUT
        #": GET A$: HOME : GOTO 9105
9320    AZ = YR * 2 + (MN > 7)
9330    BZ = 32 * (MN -  INT (MN / 8) * 8) + DY
9340    CZ = MM
9350    DZ = HH
9360    POKE 49040,BZ: POKE 49041,AZ: POKE 49042,CZ:
        POKE 49043,DZ
9499    GOTO 131

9500    REM  DATE.SET  DATA
9510    FOR X = 1 TO 12: READ MN$(X): NEXT
9520    RETURN
9530    DATA
        JAN,FEB,MAR,APR,MAY,JUN,JUL,AUG,SEP,OCT,NOV,DEC
```

```
30000   REM A.P.P.L.E. PRESENTS LOGO
30001   CLEAR : POKE 50,63: TEXT : CALL - 936
30002   POKE 24576,99
30003   KB = - 16384:KS = - 16368
30005   POKE KS,0
30010   VTAB 1: HTAB 2: PRINT "   ";: HTAB 9: PRINT "
        ";: HTAB 17: PRINT "    ";: HTAB 25: PRINT "
        ";: HTAB 33: PRINT "     "
30020   PRINT " ";: HTAB 5: PRINT " ";: HTAB 9: PRINT "
        ";: HTAB 13: PRINT " ";: HTAB 17: PRINT " ";:
        HTAB 21: PRINT " ";: HTAB 25: PRINT " ";: HTAB
        33: PRINT " "
30030   PRINT "     ";: HTAB 9: PRINT "     ";: HTAB
        17: PRINT "     ";: HTAB 25: PRINT " ";: HTAB
        33: PRINT "   "
30040   PRINT " ";: HTAB 5: PRINT " ";: HTAB 9: PRINT "
        ";: HTAB 17: PRINT " ";: HTAB 25: PRINT " ";:
        HTAB 33: PRINT " "
30050   PRINT " ";: HTAB 5: PRINT " ";: HTAB 7: PRINT
        " ";: HTAB 9: PRINT " ";: HTAB 15: PRINT " ";:
        HTAB 17: PRINT " ";
30060   HTAB 23: PRINT " ";: HTAB 25: PRINT "     ";:
        HTAB 31: PRINT " ";: HTAB 33: PRINT "     ";:
        HTAB 39: PRINT " "
30070   POKE 50,255: PRINT
30080   PRINT "A        P        P        L        E": HTAB 2:
        PRINT "P        U        R        I        X"
30090   HTAB 3: PRINT "P        G        O        B        C":
        HTAB 4: PRINT "L        E        G        R        H"
30100   HTAB 5: PRINT "E        T        R        A        A":
        HTAB 13: PRINT "S        A        R        N"
30110   HTAB 14: PRINT "O        M        Y        G": HTAB
        15: PRINT "U";: HTAB 36: PRINT "E"
30120   HTAB 16: PRINT "N":HTAB 17: PRINT "D"
30130   POKE 50,63: PRINT : PRINT : HTAB 10: PRINT "
        P R E S E N T S ": PRINT:HTAB 5:NORMAL: PRINT
        "APPILOT/W1 BY BILL MARTENS"
30140   POKE 50,255
30150   FOR I = 1 TO 3000: NEXT I
30160   GOTO 2
30202   REM APPILOT/W1
```

```
30203    REM Copyright 1982 Apple Pugetsound Program
         Library Exchange (A.P.P.L.E.)
30204    REM WWW.CALLAPPLE.ORG
30206    REM
30207    REM Production & Design - Bill Martens
30213    REM
```

DEMO.01.PLT

```
@ START
C:!01=1
C:!02=100
@ TYPE
T:!01;
M:!01=!02
YJ:END
T:'.';
C:!01+1
J:TYPE
@ END
E:
```

PILOT.HELP.MAIN

PILOT COMMAND REFERENCE

COMMAND	EXPLANATION
A:	GET USER INPUT FROM KEYBOARD
C:	COMPUTE
D:	DELAY EXECUTION FOR SPECIFIED AMOUNT OF TIME
E:	END EXECUTION OF PILOT PROGRAM
F:	FLASHING TEXT MODE
H:	HOME CURSOR
I:	INKEY
J:	JUMP TO SPECIFIED LINE NUMBER
M:	COMPARE USER INPUT TO THE FOLLOWING
O:	INVERSE TEXT MODE
Q:	NORMAL TEXT MODE
S:	JUMP TO SUBROUTINE AT SPECIFIED LINE#
T:	TYPE TEXT TO SCREEN
X:	RETURN FROM SUBROUTINE
Z:	CHAIN ANOTHER PILOT PROGRAM
*:	REMARKS OR COMMENTS FOLLOW
Y	THESE TWO CHARACTERS ARE
N	DELIMITERS FOR BOOLEAN TO CHECK FLAGS ON INPUT COMPARES

PILOT.HELP.EDIT

PILOT EDITOR COMMAND REFERENCE

COMMAND	EXPLANATION
E	ENTER THE EDIT MORE TO INPUT PROGRAM LINES
D	DELETE LINES FROM THE CURRENT PROGRAM
I	INSERT LINES INTO THE CURRENT PROGRAM
?	GET THIS HELP MENU
Q	QUIT TO THE DOS MODE

PILOT.HELP.CMDS

DOS COMMAND REFERENCE

COMMAND	EXPLANATION
CAT	CATALOG DISK DIRECTORY
LOAD	GET A PILOT PROGRAM INTO MEMORY
SAVE	STORE A PILOT PROGRAM ONTO DISK
LOCK	WRITE PROTECT A FILE
UNLOCK	WRITE ENABLE A FILE
RUN	EXECUTE THE PILOT PROGRAM IN MEMORY
EDIT	ENTER THE EDITOR MODE
DEL	DELETE A DISK FILE
EXEC	EXECUTE A SYSTEM FILE
BYE	EXIT THE PILOT SYSTEM
OLD	BRING BACK OLD PROGRAM (ONLY AFTER NEW)
NEW	CLEAR MEMORY
PRON	TURN THE PRINTER ON
PROFF	TURN THE PRINTER OFF
PREFIX	SHOW THE CURRENT PREFIX OR SET NEW ONE
HELP	GET THIS MENU

MAKE HELP FILES

```
10   D$=CHR$(4)
20   PRINT D$;"OPEN PILOT.HELP.MAIN"
30   PRINT D$;"WRITE PILOT.HELP.MAIN"
40   PRINT "PILOT COMMAND REFERENCE"
50   PRINT "-----------------------"
60   PRINT "COMMAND        EXPLANATION"
70   PRINT "-------        --------------------------"
80   PRINT "A:             GET USER INPUT FROM
     KEYBOARD"
90   PRINT "C:             COMPUTE"
100  PRINT "D:             DELAY EXECUTION FOR
     SPECIFIED AMOUNT OF TIME"
110  PRINT "E:             END EXECUTION OF PILOT
     PROGRAM"
120  PRINT "F:             FLASHING TEXT MODE"
130  PRINT "H:             HOME CURSOR"
140  PRINT "I:             INKEY"
150  PRINT "J:             JUMP TO SPECIFIED LINE
     NUMBER"
160  PRINT "M:             COMPARE USER INPUT TO THE
     FOLLOWING"
170  PRINT "O:             INVERSE TEXT MODE"
180  PRINT "Q:             NORMAL TEXT MODE"
190  PRINT "S:             JUMP TO SUBROUTINE AT
     SPECIFIED LINE#"
200  PRINT "T:             TYPE TEXT TO SCREEN"
210  PRINT "X:             RETURN FROM SUBROUTINE"
220  PRINT "Z:             CHAIN ANOTHER PILOT
     PROGRAM"
230  PRINT "*:             REMARKS OR COMMENTS
     FOLLOW"
240  PRINT "Y              THESE TWO CHARACTERS ARE"
250 PRINT "N               DELIMITERS FOR BOOLEAN TO
     CHECK"
260  PRINT "               FLAGS ON INPUT COMPARES"
270  PRINT D$;"CLOSE PILOT.HELP.MAIN"
280  PRINT D$;"OPEN PILOT.HELP.EDIT"
290  PRINT D$;"WRITE PILOT.HELP.EDIT"
```

```
300   PRINT "PILOT EDITOR COMMAND REFERENCE"
310   PRINT "------------------------------"
320   PRINT "COMMAND           EXPLANATION"
330   PRINT "-------          ---------------------
      ----------------------"
340   PRINT "   E             ENTER THE EDIT MODE TO
      INPUT PROGRAM LINES"
350   PRINT "   D             DELETE LINES FROM THE
      CURRENT PROGRAM"
360   PRINT "   I             INSERT LINES INTO THE
      CURRENT PROGRAM"
370   PRINT "   ?             GET THIS HELP MENU"
380   PRINT "   Q             QUIT TO THE DOS MODE"
390   PRINT D$;"CLOSE PILOT.HELP.EDIT"
400   PRINT D$;"OPEN PILOT.HELP.CMDS"
410   PRINT D$;"WRITE PILOT.HELP.CMDS"
420   PRINT "DOS COMMAND REFERENCE"
430   PRINT "---------------------"
440   PRINT "COMMAND           EXPLANATION"
450   PRINT "-------          ---------------------
      --------"
460   PRINT "CAT              CATALOG DISK DIRECTORY"
470   PRINT "LOAD             GET A PILOT PROGRAM INTO
      MEMORY"
480   PRINT "SAVE             STORE A PILOT PROGRAM ONTO
      DISK"
490   PRINT "LOCK             WRITE PROTECT A FILE"
500   PRINT "UNLOCK           WRITE ENABLE A FILE"
510   PRINT "RUN              EXECUTE THE PILOT PROGRAM
      IN MEMORY"
520   PRINT "EDIT             ENTER THE EDITOR MODE"
530   PRINT "DEL              DELETE A DISK FILE"
540   PRINT "EXEC             EXECUTE A SYSTEM FILE"
550   PRINT "BYE              EXIT THE PILOT SYSTEM"
560   PRINT "OLD              BRING BACK OLD PROGRAM
      (ONLY AFTER NEW)"
570   PRINT "NEW              CLEAR MEMORY"
580   PRINT "PRON             TURN THE PRINTER ON"
590   PRINT "PROFF            TURN THE PRINTER OFF"
600   PRINT "PREFIX           SHOW THE CURRENT PREFIX OR
      SET NEW ONE"
```

```
610   PRINT "HELP              GET THIS MENU"
620   PRINT "----------------------------------------
      -------------"
630   PRINT D$;"CLOSE PILOT.HELP.CMDS"
640   END
```

INDEX

www.ingramcontent.com/pod-product-compliance
Lightning Source LLC
Chambersburg PA
CBHW021025180526
45163CB00005B/2127